Here to Forever

Finally Free To Be Me

VENUS CASTLEBERG

Acknowledgements

To all my lovers, friends, and teachers along the way. I know I would not be where I am today if you had not challenged or encouraged me, believed in me when I thought I couldn't keep going, loved me unconditionally when I couldn't love myself, or saw something in me that I could not see in myself. What a blessing to have shared part of my journey with you. I feel I am a better person because you were in my life at the perfect moment in time.

To Dr. Dain Heer and Gary Douglas, I am so grateful for you both and the tools of Access Consciousness®. Thank you for always inviting me to be me and choose more.

To my mother, who has always believed in me. Thank you for wanting only the greatest love for me.

To myself, thank you for being the one to help me get the missing piece in this story.

Beyond Grateful,
Venus Castleberg

Contents

Acknowledgements   iii

Introduction   1

1. A Pisces Love Child is Born   5
2. First Love   7
3. Love Isn't Always Enough   11
4. Hero   15
5. Are We Moving or What?   17
6. Oh No, Not Sexualness!   21
7. Hopeless Romantic   25
8. Middle of The Road   29
9. Dating 101   33
10. All Alone   37
11. Floundering   41
12. Different Source   45
13. Death   49
14. Life   53
15. Rebounder   57
16. The Roaring Twenties   61
17. Finding a Path   63
18. Saturn Return   67
19. God Does Not Condemn   71
20. Mr. Right Now   75

21. Gifts of the Gods   77
22. Looking for Something Wrong   81
23. Sacrifice   85
24. Seven-Year Itch   87
25. Africa   91
26. I Like Me   97
27. To Be Loved By Me   101
28. Forgiveness   107
29. Acknowledgement   111
30. The Invitation   117
31. Part 2   119
32. Home   121
33. Being a Sexual Healer   133
34. Less Than   137
35. It Will Never Work   141
36. Love, Lust & Gratitude   147
37. Significance Kills   151
38. The Devastation Judgment   153
39. You Are The One   155
40. Would You Date You?   157
41. Radical Choice   161

About the Author   165
Recommended Reading   167

INTRODUCTION

Where does one begin to tell the story of a lifetime, or multiple lifetimes, when it all seems to roll into one? I suppose a good place to start would be the beginning. My story begins with love. The search for love. The believing in and hoping for love. The wanting love, needing love, and ultimately looking for love in all the wrong places. The following of love only to have it turn around and chase me as I ran away screaming in fear; at one time even believing that I had found the one true love of a lifetime, only to lose that love too.

Finding love, losing love, falling in love to fall out of love, in then out, out then back in, repeat, repeat, repeat. My journey has been an endless search for love based on hopes, dreams, and utopian ideals. And since those points of view were mostly influenced by childhood fairytales, my relationships often ended in excessive amounts of disappointment, heartache, and loss.

In the end, my story is one of realizing that true love exists and true love is never lost. My journey, with all its ups and downs, bumps and bruises, has empowered me to wake up to a whole new love reality which changed the course of my life. The love adventure that had been an endless external search suddenly became an exquisite journey within where I found all the unconditional love and acceptance I had ever searched for; not knowing it already existed. True love, I discovered, had been there all along and now that it was unhidden and reclaimed, would last into eternity... <u>From Here to Forever</u>

"You are like a wisteria vine in a meadow. You will naturally climb to the highest point as soon as you are able, and then offer your brilliant color and scents to the world the best you can when your tendencies ripen and the temporal and eternal spring dawns.

Yes, when your season comes,
if a tree were near your arms you would move
towards it as if you were in love,
sensing some potential of giving and receiving more,
achieving your destiny, hanging from the sky.

When you bloom, is it not clear that you will offer
so much to the world to be harvested?
All your limbs, my dear, can entwine with a pillar
of a kindred spirit, like me, and rise and rise and rise
until no one on earth can see you anymore,
for there is no limit to our height.

There are so many ways to touch the world,
if you sing, your sounds will press against
my cheek in a way I desire
if you dance, I will become the ground you bless
as happiness does for this world
if you make love with another form and can satisfy it
any sighs of respite are also mine.

This is just the way things have become
waltzing towards the heart's passions
one day, my dear, you will realize you
can accomplish everything
just by appearing among us.

If I thought you could hear what I just said
and cash that in – walk off a wealthy person,
I could spare repeating it, but I don't mind.
Yes, the real blessing of this world is simply
you having ever been.

Know that from this realization came dawn
and every benevolent wave that still
spreads out exploring the endlessness of time."
~Hafiz

A Pisces Love Child is Born

"You are the root of heaven,
the morning star,
the bright moon,
the house of endless Love."

~Rumi

Endlessly searching for love with a strong desire to understand it in all its many forms sums up the story of my life. Perhaps that is not so surprising, afterall, my name is Venus, just like the Goddess of Love. I was born and given that name by my awesome hippy mother who rode in on the coattails of the sixties. She was wonderfully rebellious and young when she had me, out of wedlock, bucking the catholic system she grew up in.

As if the name were not enough, I was born on February 29th, which makes me a Pisces—best known for being one of the most romantic zodiac signs. Although I now know we can choose and create our own reality, the one saying that has always stood out for me and seemed to be very true for a while is, "A Pisces is wonderful to catch but hard to keep." Many of my lovers would likely agree, but you'll have to ask them, as I have given in to the endless pull to swim away from most of them over time.

Now to say that I started searching for love right out of the gate may not be entirely accurate. I was a loving child to be sure. Mom says I loved everyone and would often be caught walking down the street holding the hands of strangers. Good thing I grew up in Alaska at a time people were more trusted.

Memories of my childhood are various and vague. My biological father was not in the picture so my mom and I moved to Juneau, Alaska to be with my grandparents when I was two; a land far far away from my birthplace of Charleston, West Virginia. Already sounding like some sort of fairy tale, right?

First Love

*"The heart is a
the thousand-stringed instrument
that can only be tuned with
Love."*

~Hafiz

My first love was with the Alaskan mountain man my mom married when I was three. His full head of curly hair and a beard to match were true to the hippies of that time, and maybe characteristic of someone living in the Alaskan mountains. Let's just say he had hair and lots of it.

My newfound father and I adored each other, so naturally I did everything I could to never disappoint him. Even though my father did not like people much, he had a profound love for nature and the outdoors. I will be forever grateful for everything he taught and showed me about the contributions of the Earth.

My mother is the one who taught me to always be kind and loving to people. The combination of my father's connection with the Earth and my mother's awareness and kindness towards people created a loving family. I have always seen my mom as an angel on Earth and have felt truly blessed to know such an amazing woman. I remember there was a time I used to say if I was half the person she was I would be doing brilliantly, until I realized that might be limiting myself a little and stopped saying that. The fact remains, this phenomenal lady has not only been my mother but my longest standing and closest friend. Thank you, Mom.

Growing up I never consciously thought I needed role models for life and living, yet I was as impressionable as any other child. I desired to please my parents and of course I hoped that they would live happily ever after.

By the ripe old age of five, I had acquired my very first boyfriend whose name was Steven. We were neighbors in the same wood shingle complex which had all the usual upgrades including popcorn ceilings and shag carpet. We ate mac and cheese which almost matched the orange color of our couch.

I honestly can't say why I had a boyfriend at the age of five. While we did at times walk around holding hands, mostly we played together as all other 5-year olds do. Perhaps the hand-holding and declaring him as my boyfriend was nothing more than imitating the affection I saw with my parents. Or, maybe on some level I remembered another time of love. Who knows? It could have been nothing more than living up to my namesake. Whatever the reason, somewhere this was the beginning of my search for love and it would continue for many years to come.

Love Isn't Always Enough

"Goodbyes are only for those
who love with their eyes.
Because for those who love with heart
and soul there is no such thing as separation."

~Rumi

At the age of six, my mom told me that Dad went away on a business trip; one in which he never came home from. Missing my father, wondering when he would return, I did what any young girl who was missing her father would do. I picked up the phone in the middle of the night and tried calling his work. Not knowing his actual work number, I dialed random numbers until someone answered the phone and I promptly asked for my daddy. The sweet lady on the other end asked me who my daddy was and then did her best to explain that he was not there. My mom woke up to hear what was going on, came out from the bedroom and asked what I was doing. With a quick apology to the woman on the line, who apparently lived in Michigan, my mom hung up the phone. It was after this failed attempt to reach my father that Mom finally admitted that she and my dad were getting a divorce and that he would not be living with us anymore.

Very attached to my dad, since he was my first true love, I continued to spend time with him. For many years after my parent's divorce, almost every weekend and also during the summer, we would ski, skate, hike, camp, kayak, and fish together. He even taught me how to cook a little, which was a good skill to have, especially since they say, "The way to a man's heart is through his stomach." As I grew older, I realized that if I had relied on my mom to teach me to cook, my full menu would have consisted of barbecued chicken and pizza rolls which was not going to assist in finding my way into any man's heart; not even my father's. Funny how Mom remembers it differently. According to her, it wasn't that her cooking skills were lacking. Rather, she says that is all I ever wanted to eat.

The hardest part of my parent's divorce for me was seeing and knowing that they still really loved each other—they just couldn't live together. It took me many years and many relationships to come to my own understanding that love, as awesome as it may seem, isn't always enough.

HERO

*"All your wounds from craving love
Exist because of heroic deeds."*

~HAFIZ

My first real life hero was a physically handicapped daycare provider at St. Annes. To this day I remember how present and kind this man was. One day during nap time I wet the bed. He quickly whisked me off to clean me up so that my little accident would go unnoticed. Somehow he knew that I was worried about the other kids finding out or getting in trouble.

To me this man was my friend, perhaps even the only friend I had at that time, and I adored him. I was very happy to restfully sit with him at lunch time and ramble on about who knows what. When those little green round balls were put on my plate in the cafeteria, he would eat them for me so I wouldn't get reprimanded for not eating all of my food. As an impressionable child, this was my first exposure to a real time hero. Anyone who would eat my peas was number one in my book.

ARE WE MOVING OR WHAT?

"This sky where we live
is no place to lose your wings
so love, love, love."

~HAFIZ

Within a couple years after my parents separated, my mom got a wild hair and declared it was time to start over. She packed me in the car, along with a couple of suitcases, my musical rabbit, some stuff I can't remember, and we moved to Santa Fe, New Mexico.

Money in Santa Fe went a lot farther than it did in Alaska. My mom rented a huge home with a beautiful fruit tree garden. I remember the warm, pouring down rain of Santa Fe and how much I begged to go outside without rain gear so I could splash in the water. Mom, with her protective nature, only allowed me to play barefoot in the flooding rain gutters if I wore a raincoat and pants.

I loved the spaciousness of our new house. It was actually big enough for a spiral staircase and certainly too big for just the two of us, so we rented one of the rooms to a really nice couple. I remember them well for two reasons. One, they owned a stuffed animal shop from which I acquired a few different stuffed animals. Two, if I was quiet enough, I could sneak up to their glass encased bedroom and watch them having sex.

Maybe it was the free love and sexualness of these hippies that made me curious. And what was all that noise about anyway? Maybe the curiosity began when I was molested for the first time by my friend's dad in Santa Fe. Or maybe it was from secretly watching Blue Lagoon when my mom thought I was in bed asleep. Whatever the reason, my body was starting to wake up and get turned on. I didn't know that some would say this was inappropriate. I was only seven after all.

By the end of that summer, my mom decided Santa Fe wasn't working out the way she had planned. While the money she had could afford a lot more there, she was having a hard time finding a good paying job in New Mexico. Truth be told, I was more than willing to help her pack up the car so we could drive back to Alaska where we would both remain until I turned eighteen.

OH NO, NOT SEXUALNESS!

Admit something:
"Everyone you see, you say to them, "Love me."
Of course, you do not do this out loud, otherwise
someone would call the cops. Still, though, think about
this: this great pull in us to connect. Why not become the
one who lives with a moon in each eye, that is always
saying, with that sweet moon language, what every
other eye in this world is dying to hear?"

~HAFIZ

My sexual curiosity may have been the reason I was molested a few more times over the next year. I recall a time where I tried to French kiss my parents. A strong talk quickly followed. They sat down with me and explained that this sort of kissing was only for adults. This conversation with my parents

21

made me question the attention I was getting from older men and women and wondered if it may not be appropriate, so I stopped allowing it to happen.

Processing through the divorce of my parents, perhaps I was looking for love wherever I could find it and this topic of love was confusing to me. Apparently not all love was the same. Rather, more like the different flavors of jelly beans. Sometimes it was good and yummy but at other times it was inappropriate and terribly wrong. This confusion as a child likely contributed to the introduction of my imaginary friend, Puff, who was a tiny dragon that loved to spin around on my finger. I experienced only unconditional love from him and it never left a horrible taste in my mouth. Puff stayed with me for many of those more uncertain years. Later in life I did find out that maybe he wasn't so imaginary after all. More on that part of the story a bit later.

While many people have the point of view that being molested as a child is bad and wrong, I have come to see it differently over time. My point of view is that living life is far more valuable than trying to figure out "why" something happened a long time ago. Somehow the Universe or the Divine or whatever you want to call it, has our back and is working everything out for our highest and greatest good; even if in the moment we have no f*cking idea how or why something is happening.

HOPELESS ROMANTIC

"Only That Illumined One
Who keeps Seducing the formless into form
Had the charm to win my Heart.
Only a Perfect One
Who is always Laughing at the word Two
Can make you know Of Love."

~HAFIZ

By first grade in Alaska, I was running around trying to kiss all the boys. Maybe it was to get attention. Maybe it was me trying to be likeable, as this is the time when kids started teasing me. Their favorite was to tease me about my name, taunting with what Venus rhymed with.

By the time I turned 10, I was certain I was seriously grown up. I began finding way more entertainment writing Chicago ballad lyrics on the big black rocks at the beach than I did fishing with my dad. It was also at this time that I began to fall into the ideal trap of love—the reality that is embedded in fairytales, songs, movies, romance novels, etc. etc. The endless search for and belief in The One, a Knight in shining armor, the one who would rescue me and love me forever and ever.

Between the ages of 6 and 17, I went to bible camp almost every summer; oftentimes twice a year. Bible camp is where I discovered instant relationships, which lasted for one week in person, followed by writing letters until the excitement died off. You see for me, falling in love and the inevitable heartbreak of the breakup became a way of life from a very young age. I loved the feelings of falling in love, being in love and maybe even loved the drama and heartache of the breakup a little too. Perhaps this was how I started to identify my warped feelings of belonging and seek out ways to know I was lovable. Some kids who attended bible camp learned to sing, do skits and focus on how much God loved them. All I wanted to truly know was which boy liked me this week and who would be my next summertime romance because, as a true Pisces, I loved love.

Did you know there is a dessert recipe for the hopeless romantic called 'crap pie'. Yep. The pie is made up of the idea that you have to find "The One" and then they cover the pie with the religious whipped topping that says you are not to have sex until you get married. But don't worry. When you find The One, and don't have sex until you get married, you will get to have 2.5 kids, a white picket fence, and live happily ever after. I ate the whole pie, nothing but the pie, so help me god. It's a good thing they didn't say my white knight was riding in on Halley's Comet because I'm pretty sure I would have drank that Kool-Aid too.

MIDDLE OF THE ROAD

"Out beyond ideas
of wrongdoing and rightdoing
there is a field.
I'll meet you there."

~RUMI

Maybe it was hormones, maybe it was that I was a head taller than my mom already, or maybe it was that step dad number one was an alcoholic who thought it was a good idea to introduce me to drugs and alcohol. Regardless of the reasons, by age eleven I was starting to pretend to be a lot older than I actually was. I started hanging out and cruising around with some "cool" older kids. Of course, cool being up for interpretation here.

It still amazes me how "cool" I became when the popular girls found out I had sex before they did. Of course, the bragging sixteen-year-old boy forgot to mention he had date-raped me. But truth be told, for a long time, I did feel maybe I had instigated it somehow.

Luckily, somewhere I had the awareness that the road I was heading down wasn't going to turn out very well for me. Having had this awareness, when mom announced after divorce number two that she wanted to go back to college and move to Fairbanks, Alaska, I was excited. Starting over sounded like the perfect idea for both of us.

As we were preparing for our move to Alaska, one day my mom said, "You've always wanted to change your name. If you still do then this is probably the perfect time since no one will know you there." I considered changing my name to Kelly mostly because I had been teased about my name for a long time. I'm not really sure why Kelly was the name I was thinking about other than it was just a normal every day name that didn't rhyme with penis. Interestingly, even though I hated being teased about my name and even though I had the perfect opportunity to change that with our Alaska move, when I introduced myself to the first person I met at my new school, I was Venus, not Kelly. And I can honestly say, I never considered changing my name again.

As I mentioned before, for a long time I felt that somehow I must have provoked that sixteen-year-old boy to rape me and I used our move to Fairbanks to change a lot of things. I chose to be good instead of trying to be popular. I became the well-behaved girl who was neither too rebellious nor too boring. Not too smart nor too dumb. Not too popular nor too reclusive. Not too pretty nor too plain. I felt I needed to play the middle of the road at home and at school and to do whatever it took to fit in so that I could hide the fact that I was beginning to believe that there was something terribly wrong with me.

With the events of my life up until now as evidence, I started concluding that things didn't usually turn out the way I wanted, hoped, or dreamed. Between the divorces, the molestations and then the rape, I was slowly building the walls around me that seemed to be my safe haven from the world. Unfortunately, it was also the place I lived with the ever-growing distrust of men galumphed with the wrongness of me hidden in that secret vault of my existence. It took me a while to warm up to the idea that not all boys were forceful with me and would try to get into my pants. Although I still hoped the fairy tales were true, I was actually beginning to think maybe I didn't deserve to live one. Beginning in junior high and into the early part of high school, I focused on making nice friends and getting involved in school sports. Sorting out love, boys and romance would have to wait.

DATING 101

"Love
is the bridge
between you
and everything."

~RUMI

Have you ever wished that there were a manual for relationships and dating? Or how about a class that was offered in school? Not the 'putting a condom on a banana' class, but rather a class on choosing someone who would make your life even better. Or, what if parents actually talked to their kids about sex and relationships beyond forbidding them to 'do it' until you are 13 or older.

As someone who had not been given guidelines or guidance on choosing a lover who was kind and nurturing, combined with my ongoing uncertainty and confusion about love and sex, I was not in a hurry to go down the relationship road too quickly. So my first real boyfriend had to chase me down. Chase me down he did, and eventually became my highschool sweetheart. I will forever be grateful for this relationship and this gentleman. He had a graciousness and a kindness which showed me how relationships *can* be. With him I discovered that men can be patient, caring and gentle.

For the first couple of years, everything was good. We had all the makings for the fast track to marriage, kids, and building a life together. I even received a promise ring that said we would get married someday. This was what I wanted, right? Someone to love me forever. Romance. The fairytale. I thought so and yet as we were moving in that direction, on some level I knew I wanted to experience more of life before I settled down. Perhaps it was because we were so young, or maybe because it all seemed too easy, whatever the reason, he graduated my junior year in high school and I was ready for something different.

About when I began exploring dating, my mom did too. One of my mom's men that I liked a lot was called Pop. One of my favorite things about him was that he had a knack for getting me out of trouble, often. When I was about to be in trouble for something, he would spin some story to my mom about how she was a black sheep when she was a kid so she should cut me a break. He quickly became one of my favorite people.

There was a time when Mom and Pop went away for the weekend. Taking advantage of the empty house, I had a few friends over to play games and drink my mom's tequila. Mom wasn't much of a drinker at this point, so I knew I could fill the empty tequila bottle with water and food coloring until it could be replaced. What I had not accounted for was that Pop would want some tequila before I was able to make a trip to the liquor store. Mom and Pop arrived home and the next gathering we were all invited to, which was soon, Pop thought it a good idea to drink some tequila. Mom did not like this idea and a huge fight ensued. Despite my mom's strong reaction, Pop dug his heels in and declared he was going to drink tequila anyway. I had to hold him back from the bottle while mom stormed off like a two-year-old throwing a tantrum while spouting off that it was her tequila, not his anyway. You should have seen how happy my mom was when she saw Pop pouring what she thought was tequila down the drain. Of course he was doing it all for her. My side of the story? Pop was quickly becoming my hero. The hero that kept saving me, which served as a great reinforcement of what I was concluding men were there for.

Back to my dating life, I can honestly say that if there was a test, I was definitely failing at dating 101. It became sort of like a contest and was often messy, traumatic and dramatic. That was of course until I met C and we fell deeply and madly in love. Little did I know he would end up breaking my heart badly, twice, and that it would take me more than 10 years to ever fully trust men again. But there's a little more to that tale to be told.

ALL ALONE

"... Be grateful for whoever comes,
because each has been sent
as a guide from beyond."

~*RUMI*

What if I told you that there are three pivotal times in our lives that occur when we are children? What if for all of us, these pivotal events happen around the same ages... 6, 12 and 18? For me, it was certainly true. My mom and dad divorced when I was 6. I was date raped when I was 12. My dad died when I was 18. Those were the three 'big' events and when I reflect more closely on the past, I see that there were quite a few other life-altering events that occurred at those ages as well. An example? Moving. Somehow, each of the 'big' traumatic events of my childhood occurred around the times that I moved to a completely different city. Moving to Santa Fe with my mom occurred after the divorce. Moving to Fairbanks occurred after the rape. Arriving at college in Pennsylvania and two weeks later receiving the call stating that my father had passed away from a heart attack in Juneau, Alaska while in the swimming pool locker room. There is more to the tale of my father's passing, but let's back up a little, to what I consider a couple of the most difficult years of my life.

It all began the summer before my senior year. I remember sitting in McDonalds with the man I actually thought I was going to marry. I was so happy. I was about to go visit my dad for the summer and go to camp as well. I knew I would miss my boyfriend and I also "knew" that I was in love and totally committed to him. As we sat chatting at McDonald's, the inconceivable happened. He started talking about how he knew what went on at camp and he couldn't handle the thought of me cheating on him so he thought we should break up. I was crushed. Here I was thinking that I had found my one true love of a lifetime only to have the proverbial rug ripped out from underneath me. What do you do when the love of your life leaves you because of what might happen?

What any self-respecting person would do, of course!
I went to camp, got my summertime romance on,
all the while deeply aching inside. The heaviness of
my illusions of love began to crumble around me.
Mom broke up with my hero Pop at the same time
and moved on to a very religious man named Walter.
Lover lost. Hero lost.

The fall after camp was my senior year of high school.
Still dealing with the loss of love, the despair that
followed and the feeling of being alone, my three
best friends joined the list of departures. One moved
away. One graduated early. One, I discovered, was
not actually my friend and did not have my back.
Adding fuel to the already roaring fire, I was
being judged by others in school for breaking my
high school sweetheart's heart earlier on. Home
was difficult as well. Religious Walter, mom's new
fiancé, was trying to impose rules on me that I had
never had before. With all these things combined, it
seemed like I no longer belonged - anywhere. One
good thing about being uncomfortable is that when
you get uncomfortable enough, you look for other
possibilities, which is exactly what I did. In my search
for other options, I discovered that I could graduate
a semester early if I didn't take any free class time.

Yes! A way out. I dove into school, looking forward to being done with Fairbanks and going to college.

My college plan was to study journalism. My dad however, convinced me that I needed to go for a "real" job. I listened and followed his advice. Giving up the dream of journalism and the college I desired landed me in Anchorage, Alaska, living with my aunt and uncle. I went from a house of rules to a house of no rules and no curfew. I began attending community college, working at JC Penny's, dating a drug dealer, drinking, and doing too much of that crazy white stuff people put up their nose.

When I got a little carried away and stopped being respectful of my aunt and uncle, they asked me to move out. This landed me into a creepy roommate situation and shortly thereafter I got fired from JCPenneys. Seemed I was on a roll so why stop there? I didn't. I dropped out of community college too. No job, no school, family and friends dislodged from my life, I was beginning to feel all alone in this world.

FLOUNDERING

"Run my dear,
From anything
That may not strengthen
Your precious budding wings.
Run like hell my dear,
From anyone likely
To put a sharp knife
Into the sacred, tender vision
Of your beautiful heart."

~HAFIZ

My recent life choices left me floundering without anyone or anything to fall back on and I started to worry about how I was going to pay rent. I called my mom to talk and was considering asking for help. It is possible help was exactly what I received even though it didn't look like anything I expected. In our conversation, I discovered that she and Walter, now her husband, were soon moving to Oklahoma, where he was from. With this new information, any hope of mom sending me money was gone so I didn't even ask. She also let me know that she would not be attending my high school graduation. The two things I wanted, money and someone attending my graduation, weren't going to come from Mom, so I called my dad. In talking with my dad I didn't have the heart to tell him that I had gotten fired or that I could use some financial assistance, so I just asked if he was going to my graduation. He said no.

Those conversations didn't go the way I intended. I sat for a moment, taking stock of my life and looking more closely at what I had created. Even though up until this point I was intending to go back for my high school graduation, I began to wonder, "If my mom and dad aren't going to be there, why should I?" The truth is, I didn't really like how isolated, lost and alone I felt and I was starting to recognize that I was the only one that could change that. Time to make a different choice. I called my mom back and asked if I could go with her and Walter to Oklahoma for a while.

They picked me up in Anchorage and we road tripped to Oklahoma where I spent a few months looking for a sense of belonging, and hoping maybe I could find the love I was seeking there. I used this time to look for solace in religion, however what I really found was comfort in Walter's family. Their kindness and acceptance of me was like a balm that started to heal the wounds of the past.

DIFFERENT SOURCE

"Reason is powerless in the expression of love."

~RUMI

Still searching, and in some ways trying to get closer to that feeling I was seeking, I turned to a connection with God. This led me back to Echo Ranch Bible camp in Juneau, Alaska—only this time as a junior camp counselor instead of a camper. Of course being a counselor didn't stop me from having summer time romances. Heck, maybe God was the missing ingredient to finding the One.

That summer actually ended up being a huge blessing for many reasons. I ended up being the camp counsellor of a cabin of beautiful girls all around the age of 10. One night we were all talking and sharing and I was astonished to learn that all of them, save one, had been sexually molested. The level of healing that occurred that night was beautiful. Would that level of healing have been available if I had not experienced what I did? Would it have been different if I had not been able to relate? I wondered.

That night in the cabin I began to look at the molestation that happened to me differently. What if it was a gift rather than a curse? I also began to see what it was like to be a contribution to others. Grasping this had an energy that tickled me in the back of my awareness, like a whisper on the wind, that said "This is closer to the feeling you long to have.". Over time I even started to realize that my past didn't need to dictate who I was or who I would become. While it still took me a little while longer to discover how all of that could exist in everyday life, I was getting there.

Another gift of that summer was meeting a wonderful group of volunteers, men mostly, around the age of my dad. They had volunteered to come out from Pennsylvania and help build the recreation center at camp. I spent a few weeks working with them and learning how to build.

Having extensive days on the job together, I began getting to know them and discovered that I really enjoyed their company. They were kind and had a generosity of spirit that piqued my curiosity. Truthfully, I began to wonder if maybe there was something to this religion thing because the people that I knew or had met that were actively and openly saying they were Christians, or at least believed in god, were some of the kindest people I had met so far.

I really took to one person from the group. His name was Jerry. Since we worked together a lot, I often asked him questions and he took the time to share about his home and his family, a loving wife and three grown boys. He talked about the church the group volunteered from and about this bible college in Pennsylvania where his wife worked and his boys were attending.

Since I was floundering without direction or even a home at this point, it seemed a good idea to apply to that college and see if I could get in. I applied in July, which was last minute as the first semester started in September, and I had no money. How was I going to pay for a $9,000 a year school? Perhaps a loan? With little odds of succeeding, I applied anyway.

I have been very blessed with the ways things come together for me and I often pause and say thank you for how charmed my life has been. To me, if the doors opened, I usually took that as a sign that I was headed in the right direction and going to college outside of Philadelphia was no exception. I was accepted to the college and began making arrangements to get there. Jerry and his family offered for me to live with them so that I could cut down on the cost.

The day I left Juneau was a pretty traumatizing day. I was sad to be leaving Alaska for sure, but even more than that, what I did not know at the time was that the conversation I had with my dad on the way to the airport would be our last. As he drove, I asked if there was any way he could help me pay for college. My request upset him. Apparently he had used my college money to help my mom go back to school. The deal was that she was then to help me. I knew my mom and Walter didn't have any money so I never even asked. I think the saddest part of that day was that when I left, my dad and I were not in a very good space with each other. I was defending my mom while he was judging her and I had no idea that was our good-bye.

DEATH

"Live life
as if everything
is rigged in your favor"

~RUMI

It was the second half of that summer that was more difficult for me. Not only had I moved from a state with a population of 500,000 people, completely across the country to a city of 8 million people where I barely knew anyone, I was also experiencing what the doctors called a hormonal overdrive, which caused major cysts on my face and a thirty-pound weight gain. For the first time in my life I felt I was a victim to my body and that I had no control over it.

Having grown up in a state focused on the great outdoors, a place where people stopped on major roads to let someone cross the street, no one locked their doors and where there was nothing to be afraid of except the occasional caution of bears, to a city of people looking out for themselves where everyone locked their doors, I was grateful for the care, support and kindness of the family, the church and the Philadelphia College of Bible (PCB).

It was during this transitional time that I received an unexpected phone call; the kind of phone call you are never prepared for. When I answered the phone that day, the woman on the other end asked for Jerry, the father of the house. I said, "He is not here." Then it dawned on me. I know that voice. "Mom? Is that you?". "Yes," she said, "it's me." She asked if anyone was home with me. "One of Jerry's sons is here." I said. Then the news you never wish to hear. My father had passed away. I was in such a state of shock that I actually accused her of lying. I didn't want to believe it. I couldn't believe it. My dad, who had been there for me since I was three years old, the man who didn't like people much but loved me and loved the outdoors, the man who adopted me just so I could have a father growing up, was gone from a sudden heart attack in the public swimming pool locker room. What do you do with that information? I was devastated. The memory of the conversation we had before I left for college, that last conversation, came flooding through me. The realization that I hadn't talked to him since that day... and...I was planning on calling him later the very day I received the news of his passing.

Before the interruption of that life-altering call, I had been getting ready to go to church. I could have stayed home to have some time for myself to process the news, but I didn't. I finished getting ready and kept with my plan to attend church. Barely into the service, I had to dismiss myself to find a place to cry, and cry I did. A gut wrenching cry that I have only experienced a few times in my life, pleading with God as the tears streamed down my face. "Please God! Don't let this be true! Please fix this." God didn't fix it and he wasn't doing a very good job of helping me find love either so whatever "faith" I had was quickly crumbling. If god really loved us, I concluded, he wouldn't let so many horrible things happen.

Trying to come to terms with the devastation of this loss, I actually tried to convince myself that my dad faked his own death. Have you ever felt like your life was smashed into a billion pieces? I certainly did. Everything around me seemed to be dying in some way. Missing Alaska and its unique way of life. Grieving my lost friends, my family, my career dreams and the key man in my life whom I had just lost. I no longer had control over my body. I even began to wonder if anyone, including the universe, had my back?

LIFE

"Light will someday split you open
even if your life is now a cage.
Little by little you will turn into stars.
Little by little,
you will turn into the whole sweet,
amorous universe."

~HAFIZ

The sense of devastation and loss that I experienced with my dad's death combined with the uncertainty of this whole god thing hung around for a couple of years. After my father's passing, there was to be no funeral. The pastor from my church stepped up and held a service for him next to the pond on my college campus. Just so happens it was the same pond that my wedding pictures would be taken at, but we are not there just yet.

It was during this tumultuous time in my life that I discovered that Philadelphia College of the Bible (PCB) had a wilderness campus branch in Wisconsin. Being the nature girl that I am and having received money from my dad's estate, I promptly applied, was accepted and moved on. Sweet relief. I loved it there. The college offered immersions in one subject at a time and we were taught wilderness survival classes as well. I always say, if it had been a four year program, I would have graduated. But alas it wasn't, so I did my best to forget the rest of the world for that year... which I mostly succeeded at, until another phone call, right before Christmas, that would send me spiraling down yet again. The fourth...ball.. dropped - but who's counting! The man that broke up with me at McDonald's when I was on my way to summer camp, the one I was set to marry, with whom I was still in love, convinced me to give him another chance. He was in his hometown in Florida, fresh out of the army, and wanted to be with ME. Maybe true love does last! Maybe this is it! We both agreed that although we were officially a couple, while we were apart, he in Florida and me in Wisconsin, we would see other people.

Christmas break was around the corner and I was going to see him. Excited? Ecstatic! As the holiday break was getting nearer, it was time to make travel arrangements. I picked up the phone, dialed his number and a woman answered the phone. A pit the size of the grand canyon began to form in my stomach as I waited for the phone to be handed to him. "Hello?" he said. As I listened to him tell me that he was glad I called because he was getting married that Christmas; the grand canyon size pit in my stomach got even bigger. Shock. Disbelief. Breaking up with me? Again? What happened? *When* did it happen? I just saw him last summer. It would be many years before I discovered the answers to my questions, when he called to tell me the story. The girl he had been seeing while we were apart told him she was pregnant. Feeling trapped and wanting to do the right thing, he married her only to find out after they tied the knot that this was a lie. Ouch.

The belief system I began to adopt and was committed to without a shadow of a doubt, was that everyone leaves. My biological father had never chosen to be in the picture. My mom had gotten married and moved away when I believed I needed her most. The man I knew as my father died. The man I loved was marrying someone else and had managed to break my heart not only once, but twice. Even Jesus had died and left me thousands of years earlier. Needless to say, I felt abandoned and completely alone.

REBOUNDER

"Ever since Happiness heard your name
it has been running through the streets
trying to find you."

~HAFIZ

What do you do when the whole world seems to have crumbled around you and you feel completely lost? You marry the first man who asks, of course! Now I honestly don't mean any disrespect to my first husband. We were really young and naïve to think that we could get engaged within a month of meeting, married four months later and stay together forever. But, I was still a hopeless romantic and still wished that there was someone out there that would save me from all the heartache and pain that had been consuming me for the two previous years.

This marriage, which was my first marriage, was the infamous rebound which was meant to save me and fill the void from everything I had recently lost. I had a desperate need to have the sense that I belonged somewhere and to know that I was loved and would never be left again. When you get married at nineteen, it is likely that by the time you hit twenty-one, you may discover that something other than marriage and children are possible.

The 'what else was possible' that I discovered was dancing. With dancing being against College Baptist rules, my husband couldn't dance with me. Think that stopped me? Nope! Line dancing did not require a partner to dance with so off I went. I began developing friendships and a life outside of the relationship. This choice was the beginning of the end of our marriage.

As I was moving away from my marriage, I was moving away from religion too. I was having a hard time believing God had the point of view that dancing was bad and wrong. I couldn't fathom that he was up in the sky somewhere judging me all the time while

I was having fun either. And honestly, if he was, I wasn't interested in that god anyway. Life for me was comparable to a bird whose wings had been clipped, being kept in a cage, waiting for the day when she could fly free once again.

My first divorce was not one of my more awesome moments in life. Within a year of being 21 I physically left him, even though I had emotionally left long before. Packing up, I not only took almost everything we owned, I also left him with most of the debt we had amassed during our time together. I justified my actions by concluding that because I had money from my dad's estate when we got married and that money was now all gone, I was entitled to take most things and leave the debt with him. Like I said, it wasn't one of my better moments. I did my best to make up for it by punishing myself by not dating anyone too seriously for the next ten years and by struggling financially for almost two decades after that.

Eight years after our divorce was finalized, I called my ex-husband to apologize. His response? He relayed that he had forgiven me years ago. I was relieved to hear that he was happily married, had a child on the way, and that they were setting off to be missionaries somewhere soon. Guess it all turned out in everyone's best interest after all. Not sure I would have been a very good missionary or mother anyway.

THE ROARING TWENTIES

"I used to live in A cramped house with confusion and pain.
But then I met the Friend and started getting drunk and
singing all night.
Confusion and Pain started acting nasty, making threats,
with talk like this,
"If you don't stop 'that' - All that fun - We're Leaving."

~HAFIZ

What began with country dancing ended with club dancing and every other kind of dancing in between. It didn't matter what type of dancing it was—I just loved to move my body to the rhythm of music. I still do.

After my first divorce, my roaring twenties were about dancing, drinking, drugs, and the next relationship, which led to copious amounts of sex. I was on a relentless search for something greater, but the truth is I didn't care about something greater anymore. I only cared about "feeling good." I loved falling in love. I loved "feel good" drugs like ecstasy. I loved dancing. I loved having sex. I loved falling out of love only to fall in love again.

While it did not occur to me until later, I was addicted to feeling good and maybe even addicted to the trauma and drama of life. The ups and downs made me feel alive. At least they made me feel *something* in this stainless steel barricade I lived in. The extremes of the highest high to the lowest low. Live, love, die, repeat. I really do think I believed it was better to have loved and lost than to have never loved at all.

I guess I was still trying to find my way and followed a lot of rabbits down various rabbit holes, seeking for some higher purpose to it all. Even through religion, relationships, drugs, and relocating over the next 10 years after the age of 19, I always seemed to be lost like Dorothy in *The Wizard of Oz,* only there were not any magic potions or shoes to take me to the utopian ideal life where everything was perfect and no one hurt anyone.

FINDING A PATH

"I know the voice of depression still calls to you.
I know those habits that can ruin your life still send their
invitations.
But you are with the Friend now and look so much stronger.
You can stay that way and even bloom!...
Learn to recognize the counterfeit coins that may buy you
just a moment of pleasure, but then drag you for days like
a broken man behind a farting camel... O keep squeezing
drops of the Sun from your prayers and work and music and
from your companions' beautiful laughter and from the most
insignificant movements of your own holy body.
Now, sweet one, be wise.
Cast all your votes for dancing!"

~HAFIZ

At the age of twenty-eight, I had just returned to San Diego from working on a private yacht in the Mediterranean. Still not knowing what I wanted to do with my life, I did know one thing: I didn't want to be bartending at the age of fifty and I continuously talked about that to anyone who would listen. One day a great friend of mine, Geoff, said, "Why don't you go to massage school until you figure out what you want to do? You can make good money as a massage therapist."

His suggestion sparked something in me and soon after I was researching schools, applying for a loan, and taking off to study massage at the School of Healing Arts. Within a few days of the start of classes I became filled with joy. I felt I had finally figured out what I wanted to do with my life. Little did I know that I had just begun a new part of my journey—that would shift and change over time, but would always end up with the same flavor—to help others. That realization became clearer later down the road. My fascination with alternative healthcare began with my very basic belief that something was wrong with me, that I was definitely broken and that I needed to be fixed.

By the second week of massage school, I signed up for the full 1,000-hour program to become a Holistic Health Practitioner. It would take me four years to complete the program and there were to be a few bumps along the way. What transpired over those next 4 years was worth every scrape, broken bone, and bruise I went through to get me to where I am now. But let's not get ahead of ourselves.

SATURN RETURN

"Yesterday I was clever, so I wanted to change the world.
Today I am wise, so I am changing myself."

~RUMI

There is a time period in every person's life that is called Saturn Return. It occurs when Saturn returns to the same point in the sky that it was when you were born. The first occurrence is sometime between the ages of twenty-eight and thirty-two and symbolically it is the time when you are invited to come into your own power and start making choices that work for you. It is when you begin to wake up and realize that what *you* believe may actually be different than what you were taught.

I was in school four days a week and still partying like a rock star three or four days a week when my first Saturn Return occurred. The deeper I dove into my training, the clearer it became that something didn't feel quite right. I could actually feel my body beginning to shut down in some way.

Then the inevitable thing that happens when you push your body too hard or when you keep telling everyone you need a break and you don't take it, your body says, "Enough!" and does what it needs to, happened to me. The, "Enough!" that I experienced was that something actually broke. It was my first experience of manifesting exactly what I kept saying I needed. "I need a break." Turned into an actual BREAK. I had an ATV accident that shattered my right arm into 100 pieces, give or take a few. Needless to say, I don't say "I need a break" anymore.

At the time I broke my arm, I was only halfway through school, and now I was out of work as it is hard to do much of anything without a right arm. In Spite of all that was going on, the universe still had my back and apparently a plan.

A couple months prior to this life-altering event, I was sensing that maybe I needed to move away from San Diego and give myself a fresh start. I was starting to know instinctively that I needed to stop partying, but didn't know how to walk away just yet. Colorado seemed to be pulling me, but it would be many more years before I made it there.

While recovering from the ATV accident, my school announced that they were going to give out a couple scholarships and seeing as I was unable to work, this sounded like a good plan! I made a deal with the Divine. If I was supposed to stay in San Diego and finish school, then I would get one of the scholarships to pay off the rest of my student loan. You guessed it. I arrived home from the hospital with my broken arm to find the letter stating that I had received the scholarship. What does one do when you can't work and you now have a scholarship to finish school? You finish school.

Not being able to do hands-on classes due to my injury, I switched to studying other alternative medicines such as hypnotherapy, herbalism, and nutrition. Somewhere in the process of taking these classes, I realized a couple of key things. One, the body, mind, and spirit need to be treated as a whole system. Two, my arm should not have broken quite that badly and I really needed to make some big changes in my life. Basically, I needed to quit partying.

I gave myself an ultimatum by setting a time limit on my partying lifestyle. When I turned 30, that was it, I would quit and that is what I did. I quit drugs, I quit going out to clubs, I quit most of my friends. I left it all behind. Walked away cold turkey. It was a complete overhaul of my life. Somehow, in some way, I knew that if I didn't make the drastic changes I did, I would be dead by the time I was thirty-five.

During this transformational time, I made a conscious choice to start taking better care of myself and even began cleansing my body and eating healthier. With the help of hypnotherapy, I was able to finally let go of the past and all the grief associated with losing my dad and my first love from ten years prior. My whole life changed for the better. Yet, even with all of this conscious change, there was still a nagging thought that I never seemed to shake… There is something wrong with me. I am definitely broken.

GOD DOES NOT CONDEMN

"Your task is not to seek for love, but merely to seek and find all the barriers within yourself that you have built against it."

~RUMI

Do you remember the whole guilt thing about sex that I bought in to when I was a child? Guilt around sex continued for many, many years, all the way up until the time I turned thirty, and it did not skip one single day. Then, in an instant, it all changed. Perhaps you have experienced moments in your life where something changes in a moment, in such a big way, and you are never the same afterward? This is the story of one of the days.

I was working with an amazing hypnotherapy mentor. I went to his office to tell him that I had met someone and that we were going to wait until we got married to have sex. Even though I had taken that route with my first marriage and it hadn't worked out so well, I was going to try again.

Randomly bringing up the sex topic by telling him of my plan to wait, opened a dialogue where I began to examine why I believed what I did. It was during this conversation, in a space where I had learned to feel safe and seen, that he said, "God does not condemn because god does not judge." And I said, "Of course not." On some level I knew what he said was true; that there was not some being sitting somewhere, judging my actions as right or wrong. There was not some hell I would be sent to for having and enjoying sex. I was not some horrible person who deserved hell and damnation because I enjoyed my body. Yet, how many times did I hear someone railing on about the sins of the flesh? As I was taking a closer look through the course of this conversation, I started to question things. Do I really think god, or the divine, or the universe, is somewhere judging that you shouldn't enjoy yourself and enjoy your body? Until that moment the answer was yes. I did believe exactly what I had been taught. God is judging, and enjoying sex and enjoying your body is wrong.

That day, I laid that belief to rest and I now have the point of view that we are all playing in a giant sandbox and the universe doesn't have a judgment or an opinion about how any of us play. We get to choose the life we desire and live the way that works best for each of us. If we want to play with others we can. If we love playing alone, that's okay too. If we want to throw a fit, we don't need anyone's permission to do so. If we want to bury our head in the sand, we get to do that. Now, I do believe that the divine would love for each of us to choose whatever brings us joy, but if we really desire to struggle then we have the freedom to choose that too.

After my new-found realization, I did end up having sex with the guy I was dating—guilt-free for the first time ever. Then, we broke up, which led to meeting the man I would be with for most of my thirties. As soon as I had permission to have all the sex I wanted, I chose to get into a long-term committed relationship. Ironic.

MR. RIGHT NOW

"What you seek is seeking you."

~RUMI

It has been said that just when we stop looking, someone will appear. Shortly after the previous breakup, my dear friend's brother called and asked if he could make dinner for me. Something was different about this one. Somewhere between having guilt over sex and no more guilt over sex, I finally had permission to just have some fun. On my way to dinner that night, I remember calling my friends and telling them I was no longer looking for Mr. Right. I was looking for Mr. Right Now. Lucky guy.

Dinner was wonderful. I still remember the shrimp fettuccine he prepared. Dinner progressed to making out, which a few dates later turned into sex, this time without guilt, which turned into dating, which turned into great parties with loved ones, cake fights, laughter, and fun unlike anything I had ever experienced before. We attended transformational classes together, eventually lived together, got engaged and then married.

Mr. Right Now ended up being Mr. Right after all. I felt extremely fortunate to spend many years together enjoying each other's company. To love and be loved in a way I never had before, and even believing I had found my soulmate.

Much later, I realized that there is more than one soul mate for each of us. As a matter a fact, there are quite a few soul mates, and they take on many different forms. They can be our best friends, our lovers, and even some of our families and teachers.

GIFTS OF THE GODS

*"You have no idea how hard I've looked for a gift to bring
You. Nothing seemed right. What's the point of bringing gold
to the gold mine, or water to the ocean. Everything I came
up with was like taking spices to the Orient. It's no good
giving my heart and my soul because you already have these.
So I've brought you a mirror. Look at yourself and remember
me."*

~RUMI

H ave you ever received a gift and thought, *Okay,
that's interesting, but is there a receipt? Can I trade
it in for something I would actually like or maybe even
use?*

Imagine getting the gift of becoming a psychic and a medium pretty much overnight, which is precisely what happened to me at the age of thirty. *Are you f**king kidding me? I don't want it! Take it back! I'm not doing anything with this. I will not be the crazy lady everyone talks about. I'm NOT having it.*

Well let's just say that the universe had other plans. There was no receipt, no trade-in policy, and they never did take it back—even with my 3 years of resistance.

To be fair, I had been toying with doing readings, developing my psychic abilities and embarking in Reiki trainings. However, the medium aspect was not what I had been asking for, looking for or wanting in *any* way.

When this "undesirable gift" was delivered, or perhaps I should more accurately say discovered, I was in that pretty new relationship, with my soul mate, and I had just completed my Reiki Master training. I came home, asked my partner if he would like me to work on him, and as I was working on him a spirit walked into the room. I told my partner, and with a ton of enthusiasm he asked, "What does he look like?" I responded, "It's a tall thin man with sunken eyes and a plaid shirt." "Oh I know exactly who that is! he said excitedly. "It's the ranch hand from my ranch where I grew up." "Really?" I asked. "That's cool! Is he still alive?" "No," he replied. "Fanfuckintastic! Apparently I'm a medium!" was my immediate response. The ongoing joke to this day is that I see dead people. I don't see them maimed, or see the way they died, or get gruesome images of the deceased person as others describe. I see the details that would help the living person I am talking with recognize them. Most of the time the details make sense, but every once in a while they don't. I also can't control who I see; if they want to visit someone, they do.

Another thing I learned early on is that if spirits know you can see them, they will appear everywhere. Not wanting to be consumed with this ability, I had to lay down some serious rules. "No, I'm not going to approach the woman in the grocery store to tell her that her grandmother is here!" I was also aware that at the time I was not emotionally stable enough to use my gift in certain ways such as finding missing children, even though two of my mentors had done that at one time or another. I resisted the ability to see beyond the veil for years. I had a very narrow point of view and little allowance for this *supposed* gift. I had the point of view that it was more of a curse and since your point of view creates your reality, I spent the next 3 years in misery.

The hardest part of processing this ability that I had was the growing gap I created between me and my mom. We had been close my whole life, but when I was given this gift I pulled away from her and couldn't tell her for three years. Three years was long enough. I needed to get some answers so I set out on a vision quest. Sedona, Arizona seemed like the place to go, even though I had never been there. While there, a dear friend helped me come to terms with the gifts I had been given. His presence in my life at that time will always be remembered with the deepest gratitude.

Between my Saturn Return and Sedona lots of things occurred, most likely another book all together, but suffice it to say I left there feeling okay. Not great but okay.

LOOKING FOR SOMETHING WRONG

The wind and I could come by and carry
you the last part of your journey, if you
became light enough,
by just letting go of a few more things you
are clinging to...that still believe in
gravity.

~HAFIZ

Did you know that if you are looking for something wrong, or even something right, you will definitely find it? There is this place in between, only known to some, where we discover that there is ultimately nothing right or wrong and there is no right or wrong way of doing things. You will do what works for you or you won't. You will fall in love with another or you won't. You will choose for you or you won't. Either way, I guarantee you will find whatever you are looking for if you look hard enough. You can find all the justifications and proof of whatever you desire to believe. Just Google it.

Searching for something wrong with me was all I did in my thirties. I really thought there was something innately wrong with me and that there had to be some modality somewhere that would fix it. Getting married again had to be the answer. That would fix it. It didn't; and boy did I try to make him leave at first. It's a wonderful thing when you meet someone who loves you no matter what. But even then I couldn't see the forest through the trees. I *knew* I was broken, I *knew* I was wrong, and I would use every tool out there to prove it.

The love box had been ticked since I thought I had found the love of my life, and since I was certain I was broken and therefore required fixing, I turned to the endless search for wholeness. There had to be something out there that would fix me. Little did I know that it was a desperate call for love of a different kind that I was searching for; a love for myself.

My search for wholeness included thousands of dollars, a ton of healing modalities, transformational work, classes, books, and more. You name it, I probably did it. All of the things I dabbled in did shift and change me to some degree, and I acquired many tools to use and work with in my life and business. Yet, it was forever clear to me that I was still missing something. I could always find and acknowledge something being wrong.

I searched and searched and searched. I practiced and practiced and practiced. I hoped and hoped and hoped for some sort of relief from this burden I carried like a wooden cross on my back. Ultimately searching for love in all the wrong places.

SACRIFICE

"Stop in somebody's shadow to rest and cool down, and you
are lost.
No one can make anyone else happy."

~PETER DEUNOV

When people meet there is often an image they portray. When people engage with the image of another and then fall in love, more often than not, they begin to sacrifice parts of themselves, perhaps even their dreams, to be with the one they love. *I love them so I will do whatever it takes. I will try to fit into the perfect box and be the perfect person I think they want me to be so they will never leave me. And if they love me they will do the same.* Somehow many of us have concluded that this is what relationship is.

Some would even go so far as to say that remaining inside that little box and staying with the one you love till death do you part is actually what relationships are supposed to be and if you accomplish this, your relationship is working. If you are able to coexist, it's working. I'll be completely honest with you. I'm not interested in coexisting with anyone. I'm interested in co-creating.

Contrary to popular opinion, being 100% yourself while allowing your partner to be 100% themself is the only way to have a truly amazing relationship.

What if knowing that you will always be changing could be the greatest contribution and kindness to your relationships? Would you be willing to give everyone permission to do that? Did you know that you can co-create a life and living that works for you both until it doesn't? You can choose to be together every day until it no longer works for you, and that's a spectacular relationship too?

SEVEN-YEAR ITCH

"One of the best times for figuring out who you are & what you really want out of life? Right after a break-up."

~MANDY HALE

Many people have heard of, and sometimes joke about, the seven-year itch. Perhaps you have no idea what the seven-year itch is or maybe you don't believe it's real. Regardless, it is said the seven-year itch is when people stop pretending to be something they are not. It is when the image that relationships are often based on fades away and we get to see who that person truly is and learn what sorts of things they gave up to in order to be with us. When this seven-year itch occurs, we often find out that the things we thought we wanted were, in fact, things our partners wanted.

Sometimes it can be that we or our partners don't know how to express what's really going on. Sometimes, one of us comes home one day and says we've had an affair or that we no longer love our partner. Other times we simply don't want the things we said we wanted, or the things we once wanted have now changed. One thing is for certain, when any of these events occur, it's impossible to move forward in the same way you did before. You can choose to accept all of it, start over in a new way with all the new information you have and stay together. Or, you can choose to go your separate ways.

When my husband and I hit the seven-year itch, we knew we had to choose which option was going to work for us. Stay together and move forward in a new way or separate. We chose to be honest with each other and look at where we were. The biggest thing we acknowledged is that I likely said yes to getting married because I believed I should marry a good man. He admitted that he had asked me to marry him because of the pressure of the common belief that by 40 you should be married already. Clearly this was not a foundation for a lifelong marriage. In addition to this, my husband declared he didn't want kids. I was only 37 years-old, hitting my sexual prime and thinking perhaps kids would be in my future.

All things considered, we chose to go our separate ways. In the dissolving of our marriage, I was crushed and excited at the same time. Excited to be choosing what was best for me for the first time in a very long time and heartbroken of a different kind.

My husband and I still love each other in many ways. We had simply arrived at an impasse; a place where we recognized that the things we thought we wanted together were not actually the things either of us desired after all; like a family, a house, and a comfortable life, to name a few. Leaving that relationship was one of the hardest choices I have made this lifetime. I desperately wanted to hang on to my belief in the fairytale of love; the one that says you will find The One and live in love forever and ever.

Isn't it crazy to think that there is only *one* person for each of us on this planet of eight billion people? And then to assign ourselves the job of searching for that one throughout our entire lifetime? Talk about trying to find a needle in a haystack! If we find The One, it is because we got lucky. If we don't, then it must have been because of karma or some crap like that. If we get lucky and find The One only to lose them later, there will never be another. One and done. I was convinced that he had been my One and I feared that the relationship we had was as good as it was ever going to get.

Don't get me wrong ... I still wanted to live happily ever after, but I couldn't reconcile that dream with all the other things I desired in my life more. Happily ever after. Yes! Change the world for the better. Yes! Keep learning and growing personally. Yes! Find the one true love of a lifetime that would go with me wherever I went and withstand anything. Yes! I desired it all. The Universe never ceases to amaze. I did finally find all of that in a place I had never looked before.

AFRICA

"I have come to accept the feeling of not knowing where I am going. And I have trained myself to love it. Because it is only when we are suspended in mid-air with no landing in sight, that we force our wings to unravel and alas begin our flight. And as we fly, we still may not know where we are going to. But the miracle is in the unfolding of the wings. You may not know where you're going, but you know that so long as you spread your wings, the winds will carry you."

~C. JoyBell C.

Two of the places that I have lived, Arkansas and Boulder, each had an interesting energy for me—I always felt they were temporary. It seemed that there was a reason I was there and that once that was complete, I would be moving on. Having moved to Arkansas with my husband, naturally, I didn't think I would ever leave Arkansas without him and yet I did. Where did I land? Boulder, Colorado and only for about a year-and-a-half. It was during this time that I immersed myself in studying Anusara Yoga, teaching yoga in my friend's basement and making malas.

Not having my husband with me created a huge gap for me in many ways. It was also during this time that I was hitting my sexual prime. I had always been a pretty sexual little being; however, when I hit thirty-seven … good god! That was an incredibly intense time in my life to be turned on 24/7.

While all of this was going on, I met a wonderful man who I cared about and during our eight months together he was all too happy to oblige my sexual appetite. You may have heard the saying f*cking like rabbits? Yeah, that. The only unfortunate part of our relationship was that my heart was never fully in it. Still heartbroken, I missed my ex-husband, who was also my best friend, terribly. This new man was a great distraction and at the same time the infamous rebound. Not surprisingly, this rebound came to an abrupt end which launched me into the first depression of my life.

I have to admit, until I found myself in the throes of my own depression, I really did not know much about it. I thought that if you were struggling with something, you could make a different choice, ask for help, or just be happy. I did not know, but I did discover the sort of "no hope despair" one feels in that space.

It was during this time in my life that I came to realize that I wasn't only grieving the man I had just broken up with, but I was finally grieving my divorce. I was grieving the lost hopes and dreams of a marriage that ended. I was grieving the option to have children. I was grieving the many well-made plans that were now obsolete. I was grieving who I thought I was. I was grieving the enmeshment of being one with someone. I was grieving the fairy tales and stories that I no longer believed were possible or true. And, perhaps I was grieving being alone with myself for the first time since I could remember. All of this was new territory for me.

With the internal processing of a whole lot of grief, I was also feeling that my time in Boulder was complete. I sold off almost everything I owned in preparation for leaving the country. The plan was to be gone for a year or perhaps more. Heck. Who knows? I thought perhaps I would never come back. I was hoping that with this move I could outrun the heaviness I was experiencing every day of my life.

I traveled to England, Scotland, and then to Africa. I planned to be a part of some volunteer projects in Africa that, interestingly enough, never came through. I believe they never happened because that wasn't really why I was there.

I received so many truly wonderful gifts on this trip. One of them being the realization that I could travel and figure things out on my own. I learned how to get from place to place, where to stay, where not to stay, who to trust, and who not to trust. I began to see the world in a whole new light—some of which was hard to see and difficult to grasp and some of which was filled with delight. The biggest gift of this traveling adventure was that I learned I was going to be okay. I was empowered to know that I could take on the world by myself if I needed to. I even discovered how much I enjoyed my own company. Turns out I have never been, nor will I ever be, alone.

Africa was the greatest part of my traveling adventure for so many reasons. I learned how to get around in a foreign country where most people didn't speak my language. As a white woman, I was definitely the minority. I would sometimes go days without seeing another mzungu (white person) and rarely spoke to anyone for an entire month. I had little to no contact with my people back in America, aside from the occasional Internet cafe or three-minute phone conversation.

One of the places I stayed while in Africa was Zanzibar Island where I rented a cottage on the beach. Every morning I would take a walk on the beach and just be with me. There was a time when a large group of little children followed me and brought me shells. We didn't converse as they delivered their shells to me. We simply laughed; reveling in the joy.

One day as I was walking on the beach, I had the sudden realization that my depression had lifted. I did not set out to Africa with the intention of finding healing. I can honestly say until that very moment, I had no idea that was what I was there for. Yet, that is what occurred. Release. Rediscovery. Wholeness. In this new space, it was clear that I was complete and that it was time to head home - wherever home was! Having no idea where home was, I chose to go back to Boulder.

It would be a stretch to say that the years after Africa were all joy and bliss. Yet, something fundamentally changed for me there and I was never the same. Perhaps it has something to do with seeing people in a different way. Knowing that there are still children that go hungry in parts of the world made my endless search for love seem a bit insignificant. Or at least a little less interesting.

I LIKE ME

"The sun never has an inferiority complex.
It shines the same whether above or below."

~*CURTIS TYRONE JONES*

While going back to Boulder seemed to be the logical choice, since that's where I left, it turned out to only be a month's layover which involved taking care of dogs and helping my friend's sick mom. As memory serves me, it was just me and Daisy the dog on Christmas. I was drinking red wine and dancing around to "Good Life" by OneRepublic knowing for the first time in a long time that things were going to work out far greater than I had ever imagined possible. It was the proverbial light at the end of the tunnel that I had been in for so long I had stopped recognizing I was living in the dark.

While I was in Boulder, my teacher at the time said, "Since you're at ground zero anyway and you've always said you would like to live in Telluride someday, maybe now's the time?" I spent a week of meditation on this possibility and realized yes, I would like that. I bought a car. Moved to Telluride. Onward and upward.

The next four years spent in Telluride gifted me a sense of community, friendships with amazing people and a love affair with the land. While I did date from time to time, my heart was not really in it. I wasn't looking for a relationship. I dated for the fun of it only until it wasn't fun anymore. I was all too happy to be on my own, creating and enjoying my life.

It was during this time in Telluride that I discovered Access Consciousness®, let go of the fairytale idea of a knight in shining armor coming to my rescue and recognized that there was no one that would make me feel complete. It was a time when I started to see that I was on my own in ways I hadn't realized and I started asking, "If I was not waiting for The One to show up, what would I like my life and living to be?" I worked as much as I could and enjoyed traveling, exploring and camping when there wasn't much work. I really started to fall in love with myself and discovered I enjoyed my own company.

I began to see that I had not ever been broken, wrong or bad. Rather, every choice I made has made me the person I am today and that person is someone I actually like. I would use the energy of this discovery along with the courage to admit that I thought I had outgrown Telluride to move to Maui.

To Be Loved By Me

And even after the end
I will be with you again.
We've got it made if you can just believe
you'll always be loved by me

~BRYAN WHITE

It can be much easier to be ourselves and choose what works for us when we are by ourselves rather than in a relationship. Adding a relationship back into the mix after you have had this space of choosing for you can create some challenges. Especially if the relationship you choose is one where you divorce everything you are and everything you are choosing and creating to go on the ride of someone else's life. You know, the relationship where you live and work with that person, building *their* dreams while telling yourself the entire time that we are building *our* dreams, yet knowing, on some distant level, that you are giving up you and what you desire in the process.

Yep. That is exactly what I did. To be clear, I am not judging that 16 month choice of mine. I know that this relationship was one of my greatest teachers. By this time I had the tools of Access Consciousness® combined with the awareness to keep asking questions. Asking questions and making choices creates awareness, and boy did I receive awareness! I saw how I had been functioning in relationships. I discovered what did and did not work for me. It was clear that at times I still choose to shut off my awareness and ignore this nagging feeling that something was really off for me. Rather than just accepting that this was not working for me, I did what many people do and kept looking for what was wrong with me or what I could change about me to make it work. As a result, I spent most of that first year physically sick in one way or the other and sometimes overly emotional only to realize that my body had been screaming...."This doesn't work for me!!!"

As I realized what I was doing, I began to make some changes. I started to use the tools of Access Consciousness® that I had acquired and asked more questions. I did my best to communicate what didn't work for me in some not so helpful ways. Gradually developing a more gentler, kinder way to express.

Was I totally and utterly in love? Yes I was. Did I bend, mold, staple, and mutilate myself to try to fit into his world? I did. Did it work for me? No. Did I wish and hope he would change and choose the path I was on? Yes I did. Did that work for him? No it didn't. Is either of us wrong? Absolutely not. Was leaving one of the hardest choices I ever had to make ? Yes it was. And, at the same time, it was one of the kindest choices I have ever made. I finally realized that it was not a kindness for me to stay. He needed to be free to choose and live a life that worked for him and no matter how hard I tried I couldn't be what he needed me to be. Who we are and what we choose as our very own journey belongs to each one of us, individually. Trying to get someone to change to fit into your life when it doesn't work for them is one of the greatest unkindnesses delivered to any human being. It's like dragging someone on the white water rapids of your life saying 'come with me this will be fun!' All the while you know they are deathly afraid of water.

A gift that I received on the other side of this relationship was that I would no longer give myself up for anyone. Moving forward, I would demand for me and my life exactly what I desire. This demand for living and having my life was not a choice against anyone. Rather, a choice *for* me. One in which I included total allowance for others choosing something totally different. Different realities aren't right or wrong. They are just different. This is what the kingdom of we is all about. The kingdom of we includes you and it includes me.

Relationships *can* be creative, fun and nurturing but only if each individual is willing to be a 100% and totally themselves; choosing to be together because you add to each other's lives; not take away from it. Trust me, if you're trying to get a leopard to change its spots, it's not going to go all that well. And I couldn't stop, nor did I want to stop being me.

The more we ask questions and choose for ourselves, the more we discover what is true for us. As I continued on this path of asking questions, making choices and receiving awareness, I had a huge revelation about me that I had never acknowledged before. I recognized that I loved loving others and had a great capacity to love. I realized that I would love to be loved the way I loved others. And on some level I really did desire to have someone in my life who could receive my love. Someone who would be grateful for my love and would love me too. My pattern had been to cut myself off to try to be everything I thought they wanted me to be so they would love me the way I loved them. What I hadn't quite realized was that the love I was so constantly expecting from someone else was really the love I desired and even required from myself. I really wanted, deep down, to be loved by me!

FORGIVENESS

"Forgiveness is part of the treasure you need to craft your falcon wings and return to your true realm of Divine freedom."

~HAFIZ

Sometimes we really can't see the forest through the trees when we are seeing our world through the filter of anger and resentment. Of course it's not uncommon to want to blame others for why things didn't work out. I am no exception. I am, however, willing to continue to ask questions when things don't feel quite right.

Soon after getting that I really desired to be loved by me, I hit a little bit of a hiccup. I found myself blaming my ex for our failed relationship. I couldn't remember the good times we shared, only the awful things I put up with. As a way of dealing with it, I kept myself moving and super busy so it took a bit for it to catch up with me.

One day I awoke to realize that I didn't blame him. I was actually making myself wrong for the things I made OK that really weren't OK. The difference here is recognizing that I am the one that made it alright. I am the one that chose it time and time again. I am the one who cut off her awareness when things weren't working. And guess what? I blamed myself for all those choices.

It made me sad to realize that even though I had a strong desire to love myself completely, I was still beating myself up for the choices I had made. The good news is I realized that 'I' made those choices which means that even though I was choosing to make myself wrong and judge myself for those choices, I also knew I could choose something different. In that moment of awareness I made the choice to forgive myself. I did the best I could with the tools and awareness I had at that time. Sometimes love is blind and that's OK too.

On some level I knew that holding on to anger, resentment, blame, shame or regret was keeping me from moving forward in my life. Especially since those feelings were ultimately directed at myself.

Judging ourselves and others is one of the greatest unkindness we can do. Letting go and forgiving ourselves and others, if need be, can give us the freedom we seek.

Forgiving myself was a huge gift. I never needed to call my ex and tell him anything because I knew it really wasn't about him. Energetically this act of kindness freed me up in ways I never imagined. I no longer looked back on the past with remorse. I began to remember and appreciate the wonderful times. I realized that while that time may have not been the easiest for me, I became more of myself than I ever had been willing to be before. I gained so much awareness about what really works for me and what does not work for me. I am finally being kind to me, whatever it takes.

Acknowledgement

"The miracle is not to walk on water. The miracle is to walk on the green earth, dwelling deeply in the present moment and feeling truly alive."

~Thich Nhat Hanh

Today I find myself in such a state of gratitude for the past, for the present, for how far I've come. Grateful for the tenacity I have had to live a life of wellbeing, growth, joy and abundance. Grateful that I never gave up and I kept moving forward, unraveling beliefs and points of view along the way all to create a different reality; to create a greater reality. Grateful that I was willing to do whatever it took to that end; including staying in the mud to see the lotus flower bloom.

I am grateful for my most recent relationship. It was one of my greatest teachers on how to be me and choose what's best for me regardless of what anyone else chooses. I learned allowance isn't being a doormat even though I put on blinders and was a doormat at first. I am grateful for how much I cut off my awareness from the beginning, knowing I didn't belong there even if I did ignore and invalidate that knowing for a time. I acknowledge and am grateful for my body and how relentlessly it tried to communicate that something wasn't working for it even though I ignored it for a while. I am grateful for the mood swings that were made wrong because now I can see I was just demanding more of me. I am grateful for a partner that could never give me what I thought I wanted because it helped me finally look within and to myself. I am even grateful for the minimal exposure to friends, as it highlighted for me that I really do have my own back.

I would like to acknowledge how much I did choose, change and experience in the last couple of years. Beyond grateful for all of it, including the many times I went to leave that relationship but didn't. Somewhere I knew that if I left I would simply recreate the same scenario with a different person if

I didn't get through all the distractor implants and points of view I had about how a relationship should and shouldn't be. I changed everything about me that I could change to try to make it work, only to realize that I was trying to change something that is at the very heart of who I am. I couldn't change my spots to stripes no matter how hard I tried, and it was time to stop trying. It was time to embrace me. In this last relationship, I was determined to look at what I was choosing, what I was believing, what I was holding on to, what was and wasn't working for me... to be with all of it no matter how uncomfortable it was so that I could change things and have a different reality in relationships. This is exactly what I did. What became so incredibly clear to me was that me being me is what my body and I require. The greatest gift I gave myself was **me** and choosing a life and living that works for me.

Do I still have moments when my head tries to trap me in thoughts? Of course. The difference now is that the moment I recognize what is occurring, I make a different choice. I choose the metaphorical stop sign that stops them in their tracks and return to joy; knowing that no one and nothing can steal my joy unless I choose to let them.

I am grateful for my tenacious search which continues to find easier ways to greater health, wealth and happiness.

I am grateful that I have seen success in multiple ways over these last 21 years; knowing what's possible and also knowing that I can keep going up. Things can continue to get better and better every day for the rest of my life. I no longer need or require to go to ground zero to start over and build it back up. There is something else possible through sticking with yourself and committing to doing whatever it takes to change what isn't working. Sometimes doing whatever it takes won't make sense and it may at times even feel mundane, but if you follow what is light for you, you will get there.

I am grateful for pragmatic, easy to use tools that I can rely on every day to change my thoughts and therefore my reality. I can see an even greater possibility as I choose a lifestyle that works for me through daily movement, daily studies/reading and putting money away with every paycheck. I can see my relationships continuing to get even better by having gratitude for myself and for them and by asking, "What can I contribute to make your life better?" I am grateful for a community of kind generous people who have always had my back.

I am grateful for the questions I have been asking and continue to ask that are creating even more than I ever imagined possible.

I am grateful for the willingness to really see what isn't working in my points of view and destroy and uncreate them continuously.

I am grateful that I continue to claim, own and acknowledge more and more of myself, daily recognizing the contribution I make creates this world as a better place and invites us all to the kingdom of we.

THE INVITATION

Stories. We all have them. And while the facts of your story may be different than mine, perhaps the substance is somewhat the same. What fairytales have you believed? How much of you have you given up in order to try and make relationships work? Who or what have you decided you must have before you can feel complete and be happy?

One of the keys of freedom that I discovered in Access Consciousness® says, "Don't listen to, buy or tell the story." A deeper exploration of this key to freedom invites us to let go of being at the effect of our stories. Regardless of what has occurred in your life, no one and nothing is greater than you. No matter what relationship lies or lies about you that you have been believing, when you recognize that you are the one that you seek and that nothing outside of you will fulfill or make you complete, then your story becomes nothing more than the narrative of the past that can be changed as you move towards the future.

That is my hope for this book. That is my hope for you, if you should choose. As you have read through my story, perhaps you saw yourself in some places. As you walked through my journey alongside me, glimpsing the tools I used to move from the suffering of relationships to the freedom of being me that I enjoy today, know that you can use these tools to change your reality too, and that is my invitation to you.

In the second part of this book, we will dive deeper into exposing the lies that kept me stuck, repeating the same patterns, and we will extrapolate more on the tools that are available to change things. For starters, regardless of what you have decided about you, please know that you are not wrong and you are not broken.

PART 2

HOME

"A thousand half-loves must be forsaken to take one whole heart home."

~RUMI

As you know from my story, moving around when I was a kid was a normal thing. As I got older I began to think that there was a 'person' I belonged with. If I wasn't with someone, I would think, well then it has to be a specific 'place' where I would feel I belonged. I would move to a place, attracted by its beauty or the possibilities of love. Usually enjoying the opportunity to have a fresh start, a new beginning, only to eventually feel as though something was still missing. I always felt I was moving towards something that was forever elusive and no matter what relationships I had, or how magical the place was, or how financially successful I was, or even how far I would travel there was still the niggling feeling there was something more somewhere else. I thought maybe it would show up in the next relationship, or the next place, or even a new career path that would make me feel whole and complete.

Little did I know I wasn't actually moving towards anything but rather trying desperately to find me. Searching the far corners of the world. Moving to one new place after another. Traveling around the world. Taking class after class. Dating another guy in a new place certain that it would be different this time. All the while not knowing that, what was in fact the thing I was looking for outside of myself, was in me all along. Looking for a place or a person to validate me and make me feel valued and important.

One of the tools that assisted in changing this constant seeking for something else, someone else or someplace else is a tool I discovered in Access Consciousness® called the 5 elements of intimacy. These elements consist of honor, trust, vulnerability, allowance and gratitude. The 5 elements of intimacy is a tool that you can use to create great relationships, but let's not get ahead of ourselves! Great relationships start with you having intimacy with you.

HONOR

To honor is to treat someone with regard. The opposite of course is disregard, which means to ignore. Do you ignore you? Do you ask what it is you desire? Do you know what it is you would like for your life and living? Or have you spent much of your life doing what others desire you to do, fulfilling their needs, or at least trying to? Is now the time to stop ignoring you and include you in the creation of your life? Start by clarifying what is true for you. Here are some questions you can ask:

1. What is fun for me? What things do I like to do? What activities make me and my body happy?

_____

_____

_____

_____

_____

_____

_____

2. What things did I dream about as a kid? What did I wish to be when I grew up? Are there any elements of that which are still true for me?

    _____

    _____

    _____

    _____

    _____

    _____

    _____

3. If I was choosing to include me in the creation of my life, what would I choose?

    _____

    _____

    _____

    _____

    _____

    _____

    _____

Explore these questions and begin to get a sense of things that bring you joy that perhaps you have left behind. What action can you take today to begin to incorporate these things into your life? What if you took one hour per day and used that time to do something that was fun for you and your body? Deliberately setting time aside for you is one way to start honoring you.

Vulnerability

What have you decided vulnerability is that it isn't? What have you decided vulnerability isn't that it is? Vulnerability is often mistaken as weakness but the reality is, true strength lies in vulnerability.

When you drop your walls and barriers, when you show up just as you are without trying to be perfect, when you are honest with yourself about what is true for you regardless of what others think, you are being vulnerable.

When you are choosing vulnerability, that doesn't mean that you become a doormat. You can still say, "What you are choosing does not work for me."

In vulnerability, you don't have to be right, you don't have to be wrong, you can simply be. This is contrary to what most of us are taught. We learn very early on to have the right answer, do the right thing and present an image of how we are supposed to be. Letting this go and showing up in the world without walls, barriers or pretense, may require some muscle building.

1. What image have you decided you must maintain? You may have more than one. The good girl or boy? The successful businessman or businesswoman? The good parents? The loving spouse? The nice guy or girl?

   _____

   _____

   _____

   _____

   _____

   _____

   _____

2. If you were willing to lose whatever image you present as you, what would you discover about you? Would you be willing to play with that? What if every morning for the next 30 days you woke up, dropped all walls and barriers and asked the question, "Who am I today and what grand and glorious adventures will I have?"

_____

_____

_____

_____

_____

_____

_____

ALLOWANCE

When you have allowance, everything is just an interesting point of view. Someone doesn't talk to you and, rather than thinking they should, you say to yourself, "Interesting point of view I have the point of view that they should talk to me." As you say this, you start to recognize that your point of view is not necessarily real and true. It is simply interesting, and when it is interesting you can let it go.

Allowance for yourself operates the same. If you have decided that you should be in a relationship but when you are honest with yourself you realize you don't actually desire one, or at least not in the traditional sense of relationship, rather than judging you for that or thinking you must somehow change your mind, practice interesting point of view on you. "Interesting point of view I have the point of view that I should desire a relationship." Or, "Interesting point of view I have the point of view that I won't be happy until I find The One." Whatever it is for you, use this tool and discover allowance for you.

1. What points of view do you have about relationships? Write down as many as you can.

_____

_____

_____

_____

_____

_____

_____

2. Look at your list of points of view and practice "Interesting point of view" for each one.

_____

_____

_____

_____

_____

_____

_____

GRATITUDE

When you wake up in the morning, how long does it take before you start to judge you? Gratitude is the anecdote to judgment. What if, when you wake up in the morning, rather than spiraling into the litany of self-judgment, you paused and found things to be grateful for about you? When you see the gift that you are and choose gratitude, judgment goes away and you begin to fall in love with you.

1. What are 10 things about you that you are grateful for?

   _____

   _____

   _____

   _____

   _____

   _____

   _____

2. Once you have your list of 10 things, daily come up with at least 3 more. You may have to dig deep as your list grows but keep digging!

   _____

   _____

_____

_____

_____

_____

_____

TRUST

Do you trust you? Do you have your own back? Most of us have been taught to look to others for information and answers and while we can glean from what others know, you are the one who knows what is going to work for you and your life. What would it take for you to recognize this and trust you?

1. Write about a time when you KNEW something was going to occur and it did. You did not know because you had information. Rather, that sort of gut feeling about something that then came to pass.

_____

_____

_____

_____

_____

Once you cultivate the 5 elements of intimacy with yourself, you can begin to be that with another. While this is true, don't get ahead of yourself! Do this for YOU and daily ask, "What energy, space and consciousness can my body and I be to have the 5 elements of intimacy with myself?".

BEING A SEXUAL HEALER

"I will soothe you and heal you,
I will bring you roses.
I too have been covered with thorns."

~RUMI

Truth, are you a sexual healer? Did that question make you feel lighter? If it did then that means it's true for you.

When I first discovered that I was a sexual healer I didn't really want to admit it. To the contrary, I was quite resistant to the idea for awhile. Yet, somewhere I recognized that there was something about this question, that if I would allow myself to know what was true for me, would set me free. When I did finally let go of the resistance, I was able to acknowledge the truth. I *was* a sexual healer. Whenever we choose to acknowledge what is true for us, things open up, discoveries are made and freedom ensues. Coming face to face with the reality of being a sexual healer was no different. Upon acknowledging this truth I received so much clarity as to why I had chosen a lot of the men in my life. I would find the ones that I perceived as broken and I set out to heal them because I believed I could. None of this was cognitive. I did not know during the time that this is what I was doing. You get it when you get it!

Want to know how much I suffered when they didn't heal or weren't happy? A shit ton! When they were not healing or happy, I would decide I had failed and try harder. Surely if I endured long enough, things would change. Talk about being a superior asshole! I decided that everyone wanted to be happy and healthy and I was going to take them there. I have since discovered that many people do not desire a different reality. They don't know who they would be without their trauma and drama so they would rather keep it and that's OK.

I now know that I can be a tremendous contribution to the lives of others, IF they desire. And, if they desire, they will ask a question. Some of the best advice ever to be given is, if someone is not asking any questions, shut up! No one is broken. No choice is better than another. No journey is right. No journey is wrong. It is all just choice.

1. Ask the question, "Truth, am I a sexual healer?" You don't have to cognitively understand this question to ask it. Nor do you have to analyze it to get an answer. One of the tools in Access Consciousness® states that whatever is true for you makes you feel lighter. A lie makes you feel heavier. Does your world lighten up when you ask this question? If yes, then this is true for you.

2. If it is true for you, you may be wondering… now what? What do I do with this? First, know it is not wrong or bad. It is actually a gift. Second, recognize that it is not your job to heal anyone. You can contribute when you desire and you don't have to. Telling yourself the truth about being a sexual healer allows you to have choice.

LESS THAN

*"Let's start with this statistic: You are delicious.
Be brave, my sweet. I know you can get lonely.
I know you can crave companionship and sex and
love so badly that it physically hurts. But I truly
believe that the only way you can find out that there's
something better out there is to first believe there's
something better out there. What other choice is there?"*

~*GREG BEHRENDT*

Falling in love was easy for me and I did it often. Disclaimer, I really did not know what love was. I would conclude that the bliss of sex meant something, only to find that once again, at the end of three weeks or three months, I was no longer having fun and I really didn't even like the man I had chosen or was trying to fit with. Relentless in my search for love, knowing there had to be something greater than what I had experienced thus far, even with loss after loss, tears and more tears after yet another lost hope or dream, I kept trying.

I was lonely and the story I told myself was that all I wished for was someone to hold and connect with. Someone who would make me laugh and inspire me to be more than I ever imagined possible. Someone who I could show how much I loved them all the time. Someone to share and create a life with. Someone whose kisses would make my toes curl and a touch that would make my stomach do somersaults. Someone who would challenge me in all the best ways. Someone who would share themselves with me, including their greatest fears and strongest desires. Someone who would not withdraw from me. Someone who would always step up to say, "I am here, I am grateful, and I am choosing something greater for my life and living." Someone who was already choosing awareness and seeking to be more of themselves. Someone who would not want or need to be everything for me but rather everything for themselves and I would just be the icing on the cake. Someone who was happy and easy to be around. Someone who would not need alcohol or drugs to live, but rather would want to live every moment of every day as if it might be their last. Someone who would listen and want to know others better. Someone interested in creating a greater possibility for this world by being joyful and kind.

It is the illusion of love and everything we have decided that it will give us that tricks us into believing once again that The One could exist and our happiness depends on finding them. Is it really love we desire or is it an addiction to the feelings of longing that makes us feel something, anything? What if that endless tug is nothing more than a distraction that keeps us from discovering the places and spaces where we might actually find ourselves.? What if everything we have been searching for is inside instead? And, if we chose to be for ourselves what we look for in another, what would change?

1. What have you decided that you cannot do and be for yourself? One way to look at that question is to look at what it is you desire in another. Make a list. Perhaps it is kindness. Someone who doesn't judge. Playfulness. Adventurous. Fun. Whatever it is for you, write those things down.

_____
_____
_____
_____
_____
_____

2. Once you have your list, look at it and ask, "Are there any of these I am not being for myself?"

_____
_____
_____
_____
_____

3. Commit to being for you what you desire in another and you perhaps you will discover that you are what you have been searching for all along.

_____
_____
_____
_____
_____

IT WILL NEVER WORK

"Love is a state of Being. Your love is not outside; it is deep within you. You can never lose it, and it cannot leave you. It is not dependent on some other body, some external form."

~ECKHART TOLLE

If you have not considered that you will never find what you are looking for outside of yourself, I invite you to be with this idea and let it percolate. Even when you meet a wonderful person, someone that lights you up and makes everything in your world greater than you ever imagined possible, even when the sex is other worldly and you are in a constant state of wonder and bliss, even when nothing in the world seems as though it could go wrong, your partner is simply an addition to you and your life; not the source of it.

When you conclude that your relationship has reached perfection and that you have found everything you have been looking for, something will occur and your partner will let you down. People are not perfect and putting your happiness in the hands of another, expecting them to never fail, will ensure your disappointment. Not one single person on this planet can live up to your expectations, because your expectations are not expectations of them—they are actually expectations of yourself. If you have no expectations in a relationship and you know that you are the source for your own life, therefore lacking nothing, why would you ever end a relationship? There are deal breakers and you need to know what they are for you.

A teacher once told me, "You have seven things you can't live without in a partnership and then you compromise on all the rest."

What are the seven things you can't live without?

_____

_____

_____

_____

_____

Look over your list. If something is not on this list, would you be willing to give yourself and your partner a break and let go of all the rest? What a gift that would be to you both.

You don't have to agree on everything. You don't have to like all the same things. You don't have to want the same things. Sometimes you have to agree to disagree. Sometimes you have to put up with socks on the floor and toilet seats up. How much easier would it be if you would trust that your partner is going to be who they are and you are going to be you?

I was having lunch with a friend of mine and he was talking about his relationship and how much he loved his partner but there were things that he didn't like that she wouldn't change. I asked, "If she never changed, would he be able to live with that? His response? "No way." "I'm sorry to say this but if you can't live with her if she never changes then your relationship will never work." A key to successful relationships is the willingness to accept someone for who they are, just as they are, warts and all, accept that they will never change and be OK with that. If you want a cat, you get a cat. If you want a dog, you get a dog. If you want a bird, you get a bird. If you get a cat but you want a dog and you work really hard to change the cat into a dog, you are going to be exhausted and frustrated and obviously unsuccessful.

A successful relationship is possible and actually can be very simple. Not necessarily easy... but simple.

1. Clarify what it is you desire for you and your life.

2. Wake up every day and choose to create that.

3. Practice the 5 elements of intimacy with YOU. Honor, trust, vulnerability, allowance and gratitude.

4. Know what you desire in a partner and what will and will not work for you in a relationship. What are the true deal breakers? Keep that list small. No more than 7 remember? Let everything else go.

5. Choose for you even when you are in a relationship. Allow your partner to do the same.

6. GRATITUDE! Daily! For you and for your lover.

LOVE, LUST & GRATITUDE

"What does real love do?
It stills the longing, for real love is crowned,
and then all become its willing slave.
Love creates a home wherever it is.
Love is really never in want.
True love is always in a state of found..."

~HAFIZ

Have you ever been momentarily convinced that you're in love with someone only to wonder if it may just be lust? Have you ever equated the moment of orgasm to connection and love, later to realize they have nothing to do with each other?

Ask 5, 10 or 500 different people what love means and every one of them will have a different definition. My father showed his love for me by buying me gifts. My mother showed her love for me by spending quality time together. Receiving "love" from my parents in this way led me to conclude that if someone truly loved me they would buy me gifts and we would spend quality time together. If you did not do that, I decided that meant you did not love me. The expectations of what love meant did not stop there. If you weren't willing to put everything on the line for me, you didn't love me. If you weren't willing to choose me first, you didn't love me. If you didn't ride in on a white horse and rescue me, you didn't love me. If you weren't willing to cut off yourself to be with me, you didn't love me. Let's just say when it came to having definitions and expectations of what love is, I had a few! No wonder no one really ever had a chance with me.

1. We all have our ideas of what love is or should be. What definitions of love do *you* have? What have you decided someone will do if they love you?

   _____

   _____

   _____

   _____

   _____

2. What are your definitions of lust? Have you decided lust is bad? Wrong? Still holding on to the idea that sex means something? What does lust mean to you?

_____

_____

_____

_____

_____

Your definitions of love and lust are not real and true, they are simply points of view that you have adopted. Would letting those points of view go set you free to have a different possibility? What if you could enjoy lust, enjoy you and enjoy others and nothing you have concluded up until this point had to be true?

You may recall the Access Consciousness® tool of 'Interesting Point of View." Look at each of the definitions you have of love and lust and say, "Interesting point of view I have that point of view." Your points of view are nothing more than judgments and judgments are the number 1 relationship killer. Let go of judgment, lose your points of view and discover what is actually true for YOU regarding love and lust. Uncover what YOU know about all of it and what you desire.

When someone says, "I love you" that statement equates to their definitions of whatever that means. Try this instead, "I am grateful for you." Notice the difference? Gratitude has no definition. Gratitude is the anecdote to judgment. Gratitude has no agenda. It simply expresses itself with no point of view and no expectation. What if gratitude is the highest form of love?

1. What relationships are in your life presently? Lovers, friends, family, co-workers, look at all of it. What are you grateful for with regards to the primary people in your life? Start a journal if you like! When you focus on the gratitude you have for you and others, judgment goes away which creates the space for relationships to breathe and flourish.

_____

_____

_____

_____

_____

SIGNIFICANCE KILLS

"Anxiety is love's greatest killer. It makes others feel as you might when a drowning man holds on to you. You want to save him, but you know he will strangle you with his panic."

~ANAIS NIN

Significance kills what's possible. Every time you make something significant you kill what else could be possible.

Story of my life for a long time. Boy meets girl, they flirt, he gets her number, they go to dinner, they kiss, they make out. Sex is soon to follow once, twice, three times a lady. Then one of the lovers, perhaps two, make this fun fling significant, deciding what this connection means. Goodbye fun. Hello slow and painful death of commitment and expectations.

When things are new, exciting, you are exploring, you are questioning, you are having fun. Significance is the sinking ship which lands you in the abyss of the status quo.

I'm not interested in the status quo. I'm interested in what makes your heart sing. I'm interested in what brings you joy. I'm interested in exploring what else is possible that we haven't even considered?! I'm interested in discovering how it can get even better?! If you would like to discover that too, ask for it! Regardless of what is currently occurring in your relationships right now, ask, "How does it get any better than this?" If things are shitty, ask this question. If things are blissful, ask this question. If you are alone, ask this question. If you are surrounded by people and wish you were alone, ask this question. In all situations and circumstances, ask! When you ask 'How does it get better?' the universe perks up, gets more than a little excited and says, "Hang on sweetness and I will show you."

THE DEVASTATION JUDGMENT

"A Relationship that works is a relationship that works for you."

~GARY DOUGLAS

The infamous rebound. Perhaps you are familiar? I certainly am! Heartbreak occurs. Onto round 2 or 3 or 15. In my 20's I believed the best way to heal from a heartbreak was to fall in love again which resulted in years of bouncing from one relationship to the next. While it never worked in fixing the void I had in my life, I tried for a very long time.

The hole in my heart had nothing to do with how many times my heart had been broken. Some have even said that the heart was meant to be broken and it's what you do with the pieces that counts. Perhaps that belief comes from knowing that people will always let you down in some way and as long as you have expectations of them, they will. If, on the other hand, you trust that people will always be the way they are and do what they repeatedly do, then you will never be disappointed.

As much as you may wish to hold onto your utopian ideals of relationship, as much as you wish fairy tales were true, they are based on judgments and hanging on to them creates destruction and devastation for you. You can make a different choice. You can let go of the illusion of relationship and be with what is. No matter what that might be. Be with what is and be with YOU. You are the source of your life and relationships only work if you are present in them.

If you desire a relationship, choose one that is a contribution to you. Choose a person that adds to your life exactly as they are and exactly as they are not.

YOU ARE THE ONE

*"The compass rose is nothing but a star with an infinite
number of rays pointing in all directions.
It is the one true and perfect symbol of the universe.
And it is the one most accurate symbol of you.
Spread your arms in an embrace, throw your head back, and
prepare to receive and send coordinates of being. For, at last
you know—you are the navigator, the captain, and the ship."*

~*VERA NAZARIAN*

As you reflect on your relationship history, you
likely have some that worked well until they
didn't. Some may have started with strong chemistry,
hot and heavy, only to have it burn out quickly
like a match. The spark. Then the flame. Then the
warning: Better be careful because if you let it burn
long enough you will get hurt. Then the tapping out.

Have you wondered why some work and some don't? Why some last for quite a while and others not so much? I have often wondered, endlessly searching to understand what made some relationships so good, what made some so incredibly challenging and what, oh what, is the secret to forever? All the curiosity, wonder and questioning has led me to realize one seemingly simply thing. In a word... choice. It's not just about the choice to have a relationship or not, to stay in a relationship or end it, to settle for ok or keep searching for spectacular. The choice that matters in every relationship is the choice of choosing you. When you recognize that you are all you have ever been searching for, you are the source for creating your life and your relationships, there is nothing outside of you that will ever be for you what you desire because you must first be it for yourself, then and only then will you go free. You are The One you have been waiting for and when you truly get this, you create your happily ever after.

WOULD YOU DATE YOU?

"The strongest actions for a woman is to love herself, be herself and shine amongst those who never believed she could."

~UNKNOWN

Can I say HELL YES here?! There was a time when I was asked this question and the answer was no. It was actually quite the wake up call for me. Why would I ever say no to dating me? You may conclude that saying 'HELL YES' to dating me is arrogant, and that is ok. I like myself. Yes, even love myself. I love who I am. I love my willingness to grow, to learn and to always try something different. I love that I think I'm funny and fun and make myself laugh repeatedly for no apparent reason. I love that at this point in my life I live with a smile on my face most of the time. I am so grateful for my life and that I am happy with or without anyone. And I would actually get up and shave, just for me, any day.

1. What do you like about you? I invite you to go all out! If you were your biggest fan, what would you say about you?

   _____

   _____

   _____

   _____

   _____

2. What if the only thing that really matters is you liking you and being happy? Would you be willing to choose that for you? If you made you the priority of your life, what would you choose today that you currently have not been choosing?

   _____

   _____

   _____

   _____

   _____

"This is your life! This is not a dry run. Are you living it?" *Simone Milasas Founder of Joy of Business and author of <u>Relationship: Are You Sure You Want One?</u>*

RADICAL CHOICE

"I don't know where I'm going from here but I promise it won't be boring."

~*DAVID BOWIE*

Radical choice. That is my reality today. I wake up and daily radically choose for me. I am unwilling to sacrifice myself, my life, my happiness or my desires for anyone else. I am all too aware that the only person on this planet that is going to put me first is me. Everyone on the planet has the same job - put themselves first. Seek out and create the life that works for them. I am being the demand for me and my life in ways I have never been willing to be before.

In the not too distant past, I began to recognize a pattern. I would start a relationship which would end in about 2 to 3 weeks. Seems that was the magic number for how long it would take for me to give up me, stop choosing for me again and put someone else's happiness before my own. This is when the song 'I'm already gone' would play in the background like a broken record in an old vinyl record shop.

Changing your reality starts with telling yourself the truth about what is. I recognized what I was doing and also owned up to the fact that if I truly desired a different reality I must choose to be something different. Time to take charge of my life and get the heck off of the never ending hamster wheel.

Have you ever noticed that when you begin to actually choose for you that everything and everyone around you changes? Most people live life in some sort of a cave. They are sitting in a cave staring at shadows dancing on the wall. Occasionally, one of the wall-starers gets curious enough and turns around to find that there are other people standing in front of the fire holding up paper cut-outs which is what creates the shadows on the wall. After seeing what is actually occuring, some will ask questions while others will not. Some will continue watching the shadows dancing on the wall of life and accept that as their fate. Others however, one of the rare and courageous ones, wonders what else is possible beyond the bizarre dancing shadows on the wall. They stand up, walk out of the cave ready to explore what lies beyond. Radical choice. No promise of what lies beyond the walls but the determination, resolution, courage and tenacity to explore what has not yet been discovered. That choice is what begins the journey from <u>Here to Forever.</u> Is that a choice you would like to make? Is that a journey you would like to embark upon? With wonder and curiosity? What will you discover? What gifts will you receive? How much more of you will you wake up every day and be? What if, just like me, you are The One that you have always been looking for?

ABOUT THE AUTHOR

Twenty years of seeking and exploration of many modalities assisted Venus Castleberg with acquiring various skills such as homeopathy, hypnotherapy, Reiki, Shamanism, tarot, nutrition, yoga, and intuitive body work.

Currently Venus is a Certified Facilitator with Access Consciousness®, Access Bars®, Being You Changing the World® and Joy of Business® as well as a practitioner of Symphony of Possibilities™. As a coach and business mentor, she has successfully assisted clients in creating greater possibilities for their lives, their businesses and the world.

Transforming the belief that she was somehow wrong and definitely broken into the knowing that she is complete, whole and lacks nothing, Venus invites others to discover the same. Her message is simple: "You are not nor have you ever been broken." Using the pragmatic tools of Access Consciousness®, Venus engages with clients through classes, private sessions and body work, empowering them to have and be more of themselves as they create the life they desire.